MAKING CENTS OF IT ALL

A DOWN-TO-EARTH GUIDE TO PERSONAL FINANCE

SUF BAILECHE - THE REALIST COACH

CONTENTS

INTRODUCTION

YOU CAN TAKE CONTROL OF YOUR FINANCES TODAY AND CREATE A LIFE OF ABUNDANCE AND POSSIBILITY – BECAUSE WHEN YOU UNDERSTAND YOUR MONEY, YOU CAN ACHIEVE YOUR DREAMS

Hello! If you're reading this, it means you're ready to take control of your financial future. Forget the confusing jargon and sophisticated investment strategies. I'm here to guide you through a simple, step-by-step process that can help you achieve your financial goals.

Whether you're looking to reduce debt, save more, or create streams of passive income, this guide is for you. Best of all, it's designed with you in mind - no prior financial experience needed. So grab a coffee, settle down, and let's get started on this exciting journey!

CHAPTER I

THE POWER OF FINANCIAL LITERACY: WHY PEOPLE NEED TO TAKE CONTROL OF THEIR FINANCES

What is Financial Literacy?

Financial literacy is the ability to understand and manage one's finances effectively. It's not just about crunching numbers; it's about empowerment. By understanding the basics of budgeting, saving, investing, and financial risk management, you take control of your financial destiny.

The Benefits of Financial Literacy

- **Empowerment Through Knowledge:** Financial literacy empowers you to make informed decisions. You don't need to be a financial expert, but understanding key concepts helps you navigate the financial world with confidence.

- **Financial Freedom and Security:** Those who are financially literate are more likely to set clear goals, save, and invest wisely. This leads to financial security, reduced stress, and the freedom to live life on your terms.

- **Breaking the Cycle of Debt:** Financial literacy teaches skills to manage debt effectively. By understanding interest rates, loan terms, and responsible credit card use, you can avoid the crippling debt cycle.

- **A Legacy for Future Generations:** By setting a positive example and teaching financial literacy to children, you help prepare them for a financially responsible adulthood.

- **Enhancing Life Choices and Flexibility:** Being financially literate allows you to recognise and act on opportunities that align with your life goals. Whether it's seizing an investment opportunity, deciding to go back to school, starting a business, or even taking a well-deserved vacation, understanding your financial situation helps you make choices that enrich your life without jeopardising your financial well-being. It adds flexibility and breadth to your life, enabling you to live more fully and authentically.

CHAPTER II

THE TABOO AROUND MONEY: BREAKING THE SILENCE AND OVERCOMING SHAME

Money is often a subject shrouded in secrecy and shame. Many cultures view discussing money as impolite, and people may feel embarrassed about their financial situation.

- **Why Money is Taboo:** Money is linked to deeply personal values like success, security, and self-worth. This connection makes discussing it highly sensitive.

- **The Impact of Silence:** Not talking about money can lead to misunderstandings, poor financial decisions, and stress in personal relationships.

- **Breaking the Silence:** Open communication about money, whether with family, friends, or financial professionals, can foster understanding and support.

- **Overcoming Shame:** Recognise that your financial situation doesn't define your worth. Seek education, support, and make empowered financial decisions.

Practical Strategies for Overcoming Money-Related Guilt and Shame

✅ **Acknowledge Your Feelings Without Judgement:** Recognise that emotions related to money are natural and human. By accepting them, you can begin to work through them.

🌳 **Understand the Root Cause:** Reflect on what might have caused these feelings. Was it a specific event or a learned behavior from childhood? Understanding the root can lead to healing.

📚 **Educate Yourself:** Often, guilt and shame come from a lack of understanding. Educate yourself about personal finance to gain control and confidence.

📖 **Set Realistic Goals and Expectations:** Break your financial journey into small, achievable steps. Celebrate progress and understand that setbacks are part of the process.

👱 **Seek Professional Guidance if Needed:** Sometimes, money-related guilt and shame can be overwhelming. Financial counsellors or therapists who specialise in this area can provide personalised strategies.

🎤 **Talk Openly About Money with Trusted People:** Breaking the silence and sharing your feelings with friends or family can lighten the burden and foster support.

💵 **Create a Budget and Follow It:** Having a clear plan for your money can reduce anxiety and guilt. It's about control and making conscious decisions.

➕ **Focus on Positive Behaviour Change:** Identify one or two financial habits you'd like to change and focus on them. Incremental change can lead to significant progress over time.

😍 **Practice Self-Compassion:** Understand that financial mistakes are human. What matters is how you move forward, not what has happened in the past.

🧑 **Align Money with Your Values:** Make financial choices that align with what's important to you. This connection can make managing money a more positive experience.

📱 **Avoid Unnecessary Comparisons:** Your financial journey is personal. Avoid comparing yourself to others, as it often leads to unwarranted guilt or shame.

🎆 **Build an Emergency Fund:** Having some financial cushion can alleviate stress and feelings of insecurity, thereby reducing guilt or shame related to financial vulnerabilities.

UNDERSTANDING YOUR MONEY MINDSET: EXPLORING YOUR RELATIONSHIP WITH MONEY

Your money mindset is your unique set of beliefs and attitudes towards money. It shapes how you earn, spend, save, and invest.

Identifying Your Money Mindset: Are you a spender or a saver? Do you see money as a source of stress or a tool for freedom? Understanding your money mindset is the first step towards financial wellness.

How It Shapes Your Financial Behaviour: Your money mindset affects all your financial decisions. A fear-based mindset might lead to hoarding money, while an abundance mindset might foster generous spending and investing.

Changing a Negative Money Mindset: Recognising unhelpful beliefs allows you to reshape them. Education, reflection, and professional guidance can help create a more balanced and positive money mindset.

Aligning Money with Values: Your relationship with money should reflect your life's values and goals. Alignment leads to satisfaction and financial well-being.

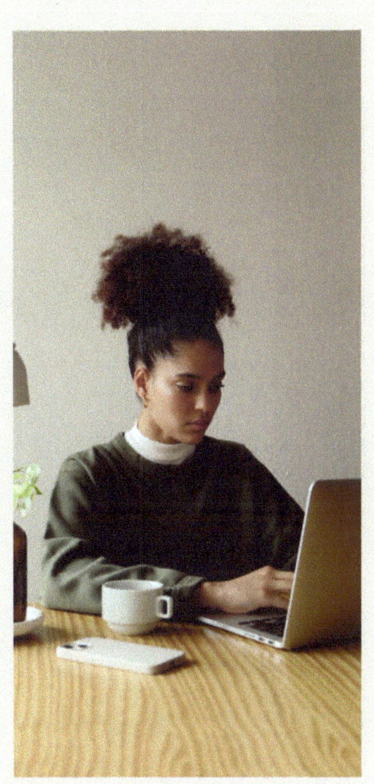

How Your Upbringing Can Affect Your Money Mindset

Upbringing plays a crucial role in shaping an individual's money mindset. The financial behaviours and attitudes we observe in our parents and caregivers often become deeply ingrained. If money was always a source of stress or conflict in the household, one might grow up with anxiety around finances. Conversely, if money was managed responsibly and discussed openly, this can lead to a more confident and positive approach to personal finance. The lessons learned, both spoken and unspoken, during those formative years can create lifelong beliefs and habits around money. Unraveling these patterns and understanding their origin can be key to reshaping one's financial behaviours and building a healthier relationship with money.

How to figure out how your upbringing may have shaped your financial attitude

Reflect on your childhood experiences: Think back to your earliest memories of money and how it was talked about in your household. Did your parents discuss financial matters openly, or was it considered a taboo topic? Did your family prioritise saving or spending?

Consider the role models in your life: Identify the people in your life who influenced your financial beliefs and behaviours. Was it your parents, grandparents, or other relatives? What attitudes did they have towards money, and how did they handle financial decisions?

Analyse your family's financial situation: Look at your family's financial situation growing up. Did you experience financial hardships or abundance? How did your family cope with these situations? Did they have a budget or financial plan?

Examine your education: Evaluate what you learned about money in school, and how this may have impacted your financial beliefs. Did you receive formal education on financial literacy or did you have to learn through experience? Did you have access to financial resources, such as books or seminars?

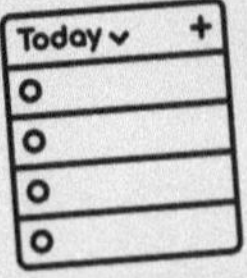

Identify your current habits: Take a closer look at your current financial habits and attitudes towards money. Are there patterns or beliefs that you've carried over from your upbringing? Are there any financial behaviours you'd like to change?

Try to seek out outside perspectives: Talk to other people, such as friends and relatives about their own experiences with money and compare them to your own. You can also seek some professional guidance or counselling if you need help addressing any negative beliefs or behaviours you've identified.

OUR RELATIONSHIP WITH MONEY: UNDERSTANDING EMOTIONAL SPENDING

Just like comfort food can be a response to emotional stress, spending money can have emotional triggers as well. This chapter aims to help you identify emotional spending, understand its underlying causes, and learn strategies to overcome this behaviour. It's not just about controlling spending; it's about building a healthier relationship with money.

WHAT IS EMOTIONAL SPENDING?

Emotional spending happens when you buy something driven by feelings rather than needs or rational thought. It could be shopping to celebrate, to feel better after a bad day, or even to keep up with social pressures. While it may provide temporary satisfaction, it often leads to financial strain or even debt.

Recognise Your Triggers

Understanding what triggers emotional spending for you is the first step to managing it.

To-Do Task:

- Keep a spending diary for a month.
- Note down what you bought, how much it cost, and how you felt before and after the purchase.
- Look for patterns and identify your personal triggers.

PRACTICAL STRATEGIES TO OVERCOME EMOTIONAL SPENDING

Set Clear Goals & Budgets: Knowing what you're working towards can keep you focused. A budget gives you boundaries and clarity.

Implement a Cooling Off Period: Wait a day or two before making a non-essential purchase. Often, the urge will pass. I just want to mention that IT'S OKAY to spend on your 'wants' once in a while - it's when it's getting you in debt is when it starts becoming a problem.

Seek Professional Help if Needed: Sometimes, emotional spending is a sign of deeper emotional issues, and professional counselling can be beneficial.

Find Alternative Coping Mechanisms: Instead of shopping, engage in hobbies or activities that don't cost money (or low cost activities) but fulfil you emotionally. It could be in the creative field, reading, visiting National Parks, cooking, video games - whatever floats your boat!

Use Cash Instead of Card: Physically handing over cash can make the spending more "real" and help you think twice. Some establishments are cashless nowadays. If you're concerned that more & more businesses are becoming cashless, you could opt for a second current account where you transfer your 'spending money' at the start of the month and ONLY take that card out with you. Bills/expenses/essentials/salary to be controlled with your main current account.

Top 5 Mistakes to Avoid:

1. **Ignoring the Problem:** Denying or downplaying emotional spending won't make it go away.
2. **Lack of Communication with Partner:** If you share finances with someone, it's crucial to be open about spending habits.
3. **Setting Unrealistic Expectations:** Too strict of a budget may lead to failure and discouragement.
4. **Substituting One Addiction for Another:** Replacing emotional spending with another potentially harmful behaviour doesn't address the root issue.
5. **Expecting Instant Change:** Building a healthy relationship with money takes time and effort.

Emotional spending is a complex issue tied to our feelings, desires, and societal pressures. By understanding its nature, recognizing triggers, implementing practical strategies, and avoiding common mistakes, you can create a more mindful and empowering relationship with your money.

Remember, it's not about depriving yourself but about making conscious, purposeful decisions with your finances. Embrace the journey, and know that each step forward is a move toward financial wellness and emotional wellbeing.

CHAPTER IV

MAKING MONEY WORK FOR YOU: STRATEGIES FOR SAVING, INVESTING, AND PLANNING FOR THE FUTURE

What's Coming In & Coming Out?

The first step in taking control of your financial future is to understand your current situation. Let's break it down into simple terms:

To-Do Task:
- List all your monthly income sources.
- List all your monthly expenses.
- Subtract your total expenses from your total income to see what's left.

Now, don't be disheartened if the number doesn't look great at first. We're here to fix that! Understanding where your money is going is the first step in making better decisions.

Needs vs. Wants

It's essential to distinguish between what you need and what you want.

To-Do Task:
- Go through your expenses list and categorise each item as a "need" or a "want."
- Consider cutting back on some of the "wants" to increase your savings or pay down debt.

Saving: Simple & Smart

The Importance of an Emergency Fund
Life can throw us unexpected curveballs. Having an emergency fund can help you tackle those surprises without derailing your financial goals.

To-Do Task:
- Determine a target amount for your emergency fund (a common goal is 3-6 months of living expenses).
- Open a separate savings account specifically for this fund.
- Start contributing regularly.

Smart Saving Habits

The secret to saving isn't making more money; it's about managing what you have better.

To-Do Task:
- Identify areas where you can cut back without sacrificing your lifestyle.
- Automate your savings to make it effortless (there are even apps that can help with this!)
- Review your progress monthly.

Investing in Yourself

Investing isn't just about stocks and bonds. Investing in yourself is just as crucial, and it can lead to personal and financial growth.

Education and Skills

Learning new skills can open doors to better-paying jobs or even a fulfilling hobby that could turn into a side income.

To-Do Task:
- Identify areas where you would like to grow.
- Look for free or affordable courses or workshops to expand your knowledge.
- Commit to lifelong learning.

Health and Wellness

Your health is your wealth. Investing time in exercise, proper nutrition, and mental wellness can pay off in many ways.

To-Do Task:
- Create a simple exercise routine.
- Consider meal planning to save money and eat healthier.
- Make time for relaxation and hobbies you enjoy.

Staying Motivated & On Track

Achieving financial wellness is a marathon, not a sprint. Stay focused and motivated with these strategies:

Find a Money Buddy

Having someone to share your journey with can make it more enjoyable.

To-Do Task:
- Find a friend or family member with similar financial goals.
- Schedule regular check-ins to discuss progress, challenges, and successes.

Celebrate Milestones

Reward yourself for achieving small goals along the way.

To-Do Task:
- Set milestones in your financial journey.
- Plan small, affordable rewards for reaching those milestones.

BUILDING PASSIVE INCOME STREAMS

Building passive income streams is like planting seeds for your financial garden. Some will sprout quickly, providing quick income, while others take time to grow but yield long-term benefits. Here, we'll explore six fantastic opportunities for both scenarios, along with step-by-step instructions and tips for success.

 **Sell Digital Products:** Identify your skills or knowledge area. Create e-books, templates or design work. Use platforms like Etsy or Gumroad to sell (or set up your own website through places like Wix).

Tips for Success:
- Provide exceptional value
- Promote on social media
- Keep updating your products

 **Rent Your Property on Airbnb:** If you have a spare room that you don't use, you could rent it out on a permanent basis or use it for Airbnb bookings.

Tips for Success:
- Be responsive to guests
- Offer unique or personalised experiences
- Keep the place clean and maintained

 **Create & Sell Online Courses:** Identify a subject you're skilled in. Plan & record the course. Use a platform like Udemy to host.

Tips for Success:
- Provide real value & actionable knowledge.
- Encourage reviews.
- Keep updating your products

Write a book: Write a book on something you're passionate about/have great knowledge in! Consider self-publishing platforms like Amazon Kindle Direct Publishing. Create a marketing plan.

Tips for Success:
- Focus on quality content
- Encourage reviews.
- Keep updating your products

 **Top 5 Mistakes People Make:**

1. **Lack of Research:** Jumping into an opportunity without understanding the market, competition, or required skills.
2. **Overextending Themselves:** Trying to manage too many income streams at once, leading to burnout or neglect.
3. **Ignoring Taxes:** Not understanding the tax implications of additional income streams.
4. **Expecting Quick Success:** Being unrealistic about the time and effort required to build successful income streams.
5. **Failure to Adapt:** Not staying current with trends, updates, and changes in the market or field.

Dividend Stock Investing:
Dividend stock investing involves buying shares of companies that pay dividends to their shareholders. Dividends are a portion of the company's profits that are distributed regularly to investors. This strategy can provide a steady income stream, and here's how to go about it.

<u>How to Set Up:</u>
1. **Research Dividend-Paying Companies:** Look for companies with a solid history of paying dividends. Strong, well-established companies are often more likely to provide consistent dividend payments.
2. **Open a Brokerage Account:** Choose a brokerage that offers access to the stock markets where the dividend-paying companies are listed.
3. **Purchase Dividend Stocks:** You can purchase stocks individually or through dividend-focused mutual funds or ETFs (Exchange Traded Funds).

<u>Tips for Success:</u>
1. **Diversify Your Portfolio:** Don't put all your eggs in one basket. Spread your investments across different sectors and companies to mitigate risks.
2. **Reinvest Dividends:** Consider using your dividends to purchase additional shares. This strategy, known as dividend reinvestment, allows your investment to grow more quickly through compounding.
3. **Consult with a Financial Professional if Needed**: If you're new to investing or unsure about the best strategy for your situation, seeking professional advice can be beneficial. Again, there are apps that can help!
4. **Understand Tax Implications:** Different countries have varying tax rules for dividends. Understanding these can help you make the most tax-efficient decisions.
5. **Monitor Your Investments:** Regularly review your portfolio and make necessary adjustments in line with your investment goals and risk tolerance.

<u>Potential Pitfalls to Avoid:</u>
1. **Chasing High Dividend Yields:** A high dividend yield might be a sign of financial distress in the company, so it's vital to look at other financial health indicators.
2. **Ignoring Growth Potential:** Balancing dividend income with potential stock price appreciation can maximise your total returns.
3. **Lack of Research:** Investing without proper understanding or analysis of the company can lead to unexpected risks.

Dividend stock investing can be a rewarding way to generate passive income, especially when approached with careful planning and consideration. By following these guidelines, you can build a dividend portfolio that aligns with your financial goals and risk tolerance. Always remember that all investments carry some level of risk, so make decisions that fit your unique financial situation and consult with a professional if needed.

PLANNING FOR THE FUTURE

Living life to the fullest is essential for us humans to thrive. You may be an impulsive person and always be 'in the moment' and that's a great mantra to live by BUT it's essential you plan for your future. You do not want to be in a situation where money is preventing you from a fulfilling life. You only live once (cliché, I know) and who wants to live a life with stress & worry? I know I don't!

Life's significant milestones, such as buying a home, getting married, or retiring, have unique financial implications. Being in the UK, various systems, benefits, and considerations apply. Planning ahead for these events can help make these transitions smooth and financially sound.

 **Buying a Home:**

Save for a Deposit: Consider a Lifetime ISA to save for your first home.
Understand Mortgage Options: Fixed-rate, tracker, or standard variable rate mortgages are common in the UK.*
Consider Stamp Duty: This tax might apply when purchasing property.

Fixed rate - Your monthly payments stay the same for a set period (e.g., 2, 5, or 10 years), no matter what happens to interest rates, making it easier to budget.

Tracker - Your interest rate 'tracks' another interest rate (usually the Bank of England base rate) and goes up or down with it, so your monthly payments can vary.

Standard Variable - The lender's standard interest rate, which can go up or down at any time, meaning your monthly payments can fluctuate, usually influenced by the lender's business decisions or broader economic conditions.

 **Getting Married:**

Budget Wisely: Be clear about what you can afford and prioritise spending.
Legal Implications: Marriage can affect taxes, inheritance, and pensions. Understand them so you can effectively budget for your future with your new spouse!

 **Starting a Family:**

Plan for Parental Leave: Understand your entitlements for Statutory Maternity Pay (SMP) or Shared Parental Leave and Pay. If you're employed, your HR team/manager will be able to guide to you to your company's policy.
Consider Childcare Costs: These can be significant. Schemes like Tax-Free Childcare may help. Again, your employer may offer some parental benefits too.

PLANNING FOR THE FUTURE CONT...

 **Retiring:**

Understand State Pensions: Familiarise yourself with the UK State Pension system and your eligibility. Find out more here.

Private Pensions: Consider workplace pensions (legal requirement), personal pensions, or Self-Invested Personal Pensions (SIPPs). There are tax benefits to putting more into your pension too!

Access Your Lifestyle Needs: Plan your retirement budget according to the lifestyle you envisage.

 **Higher Education:**

Consider Tuition Fees and Living Costs: University education costs vary across the UK.

Explore Funding Options: Look into grants, scholarships, or student loans.

Explore Other Avenues: Going to university is *not* the only way to secure a fulfilling job. Think about apprenticeships or entry-level roles that do not require a degree. Google successful people who didn't continue to higher education - you may be surprised...

 **Unexpected Life Changes:**

Build an Emergency Fund: This can help you manage unexpected life events like job loss or health issues. Usually people try to save between 3 & 6 months of living expenses.

Consider Insurance: Income protection or critical illness cover can provide financial security.

 **To-Do Task:**

Create Specific Savings Goals: Have separate savings goals for different life events and consider UK-specific options like ISAs or pensions. If you're outside of the UK, look at the country-specific help on offer.

Consult with a UK Financial Adviser if Needed: Professional guidance can be tailored to your individual situation and the UK context.

Planning for major life events in the UK involves understanding the specific financial systems, benefits, and obligations that apply. From home buying to retirement, considering UK-specific aspects can help you navigate these significant life milestones with confidence and financial security.

By integrating this information into your overall financial plan, you'll be well-prepared to embrace life's big moments, knowing that your financial well-being is taken care of.

INSURANCE: DO I NEED IT?

Insurance isn't the most exciting topic, but it's essential for financial stability. It's about managing risks and ensuring that unexpected events don't derail your financial plans.

Understanding Different Types of Insurance

Health Insurance: Protects against high medical costs for those in countries that don't provide free healthcare.

Life Insurance: Provides for your loved ones in case of your death.

Property Insurance: Covers damage to your home or car.

Tips for Choosing Insurance

Understand Your Needs: Different life stages require different coverage.

Shop Around: Comparing quotes can save money.

Review Regularly: As life changes, so do your insurance needs.

CHAPTER V

UNDERSTANDING CREDIT: USE IT WISELY

Credit is an essential tool in modern financial life. It allows for flexibility in purchasing, can help in emergencies, and plays a vital role in building a financial reputation. However, it comes with responsibilities. Misusing credit can lead to a spiral of debt that affects every aspect of your life. In this chapter, we'll explore what credit is, the difference between good and bad debt, and how to use credit wisely.

What is Credit?

Credit is the trust that allows one party to provide money or resources to another party, with the understanding that the money will be paid back later, often with interest. This can come in various forms, including credit cards, loans, or mortgages.

 **"Good" Debt:**

Good debt is often seen as an investment that will grow in value or generate long-term income. For example:

- **Education Loans:** Borrowing to invest in education can lead to a better-paying job.
- **Mortgages:** While a mortgage is a debt, it allows you to buy a home that might appreciate in value.

 **"Bad" Debt:**

Bad debt often comes from borrowing to purchase depreciating assets or things that don't generate long-term value. Examples include:

- **Credit Card Debt for Non-Essentials:** Buying luxury items that you can't afford and then carrying a balance can lead to crippling interest payments.
- **Payday Loans:** These high-interest loans can trap you in a cycle of debt.

<u>**How Debt Affects Your Life**</u>

- **Stress and Anxiety:** Constantly worrying about paying off debt can affect mental well-being.
- **Limited Financial Freedom:** High debt levels can limit your ability to save, invest, or even buy necessary items.
- **Credit Score Impact:** Mismanaging debt can negatively impact your credit score, affecting everything from getting a mortgage to your employment prospects.

Tips for Using Credit Wisely

Understand Terms and Conditions: Always read the fine print when applying for credit cards or loans.

Pay on Time: Paying bills on time will help you avoid late fees and protect your credit score.

Avoid Unnecessary Debt: Consider if you really need what you're purchasing on credit, especially if it's a depreciating asset.

Build an Emergency Fund: Having savings can help you avoid reaching for a credit card in emergencies.

Credit can be a powerful tool if used wisely. Understanding the difference between good and bad debt, and knowing how to manage credit, can lead to financial stability and success. It's not about avoiding debt entirely; it's about knowing how to leverage it effectively without letting it take control of your life.

CHAPTER VI

GET OUT OF DEBT: TIPS TO HELP YOU OVERCOME THE DEBT SPIRAL

What's Coming In & Coming Out?

The first step in taking control of your financial future is to understand your current situation. Let's break it down into simple terms:

To-Do Task:
- List all your monthly income sources.
- List all your monthly expenses.
- Subtract your total expenses from your total income to see what's left.

Now, don't be disheartened if the number doesn't look great at first. We're here to fix that! Understanding where your money is going is the first step in making better decisions.

Needs vs. Wants

It's essential to distinguish between what you need and what you want.

To-Do Task:
- Go through your expenses list and categorise each item as a "need" or a "want."
- Consider cutting back on some of the "wants" to increase your savings or pay down debt.

Saving: Simple & Smart

The Importance of an Emergency Fund
Life can throw us unexpected curveballs. Having an emergency fund can help you tackle those surprises without derailing your financial goals.

To-Do Task:
- Determine a target amount for your emergency fund (a common goal is 3-6 months of living expenses).
- Open a separate savings account specifically for this fund.
- Start contributing regularly.

Smart Saving Habits

The secret to saving isn't making more money; it's about managing what you have better.

To-Do Task:
- Identify areas where you can cut back without sacrificing your lifestyle.
- Automate your savings to make it effortless (there are even apps that can help with this!)
- Review your progress monthly.

THE ROAD TO DEBT FREEDOM

Debt can feel like a heavy burden, but it's possible to lighten that load! Let's create a roadmap to debt freedom.

Snowball or Avalanche?
You might have heard of the "debt snowball" or "debt avalanche" methods. They're not as complicated as they sound!

Snowball Method:
Pay off your smallest debts first, then roll the payments into the next smallest.

Avalanche Method:
Pay off the highest interest rate debt first, then roll the payments into the next highest.

Here's a hypothetical example showing the calculations for both the Snowball and Avalanche methods for someone with 3 credit cards and 2 loans, totalling £25,000. We'll assume the individual has £500 available each month to put towards debt repayment and each has a minimum monthly payment of £50.

Credit Card A	£3,000	15%
Credit Card B	£5,000	18%
Credit Card C	£2,000	20%
Loan 1	£10,000	10%
Loan 2	£5,000	12%

THE ROAD TO DEBT FREEDOM CONT...

Order of Payments:

Credit Card C

Credit Card A

Credit Card B

Loan 2

Loan 1

Length of time to clear: 55 months

Order of Payments:

Credit Card C

Credit Card B

Credit Card A

Loan 2

Loan 1

Length of time to clear: 53 months

Snowball Method - 12 Month Payment Plan

Month	Credit Card C	Credit Card A	Credit Card B	Loan 2	Loan 1
1	£300	£50	£50	£50	£50
2	£300	£50	£50	£50	£50
3	£300	£50	£50	£50	£50
4	£300	£50	£50	£50	£50
5	£300	£50	£50	£50	£50
6	£300	£50	£50	£50	£50
7	£200	£150	£50	£50	£50
8	£0	£350	£50	£50	£50
9	£0	£350	£50	£50	£50
10	£0	£350	£50	£50	£50
11	£0	£350	£50	£50	£50
12	£0	£350	£50	£50	£50

Please note that the tables have been truncated after 12 months, and the actual payments would continue beyond that point, following the same pattern of paying off each debt entirely before moving to the next. The exact order and distribution of payments would depend on the balances, interest rates, and the specific method (Snowball vs. Avalanche) being followed.

Avalanche Method – 12 Month Payment Plan

Month	Credit Card C	Credit Card B	Credit Card A	Loan 2	Loan 1
1	£300	£50	£50	£50	£50
2	£300	£50	£50	£50	£50
3	£300	£50	£50	£50	£50
4	£300	£50	£50	£50	£50
5	£300	£50	£50	£50	£50
6	£300	£50	£50	£50	£50
7	£200	£150	£50	£50	£50
8	£0	£350	£50	£50	£50
9	£0	£350	£50	£50	£50
10	£0	£350	£50	£50	£50
11	£0	£350	£50	£50	£50
12	£0	£350	£50	£50	£50

With the Avalanche Method, you're tackling the debts with the highest interest rates first. Since Credit Card C has the highest APR, you pay it off first and then move on to Credit Card B. By doing this, you minimise the amount of interest paid over the life of the debts.

*These tables are highly simplified and should be seen as illustrative rather than definitive. Always consult with a financial professional for detailed planning tailored to your specific financial situation.

CHAPTER VII

GLOSSARY: A SUMMARY OF ALL THE JARGON!

APR (Annual Percentage Rate): The total cost of borrowing money annually, including interest and fees.

ARR (Accounting Rate of Return): A calculation used to determine profitability, considering average annual profit compared to initial cost.

Balance Transfer: Moving the outstanding balance from one credit card to another for a lower interest rate.

Bankruptcy: A legal process declaring inability to pay debts. Has serious consequences on future borrowing.

Budget: A plan outlining expected income and expenses for managing money.

Collateral: An asset securing a loan, which may be taken if the borrower can't repay.

Compound Interest: Interest calculated on the initial principal and accumulated interest, affecting what you owe or earn.

Credit Card: A card to borrow money up to a limit, requiring payback with interest if not cleared monthly.

Credit Limit: The maximum amount you can borrow on a credit card or overdraft.

Credit Report: A detailed report of your credit history, assessing creditworthiness.

Credit Score: A numerical rating for lenders to decide how risky it is to lend you money.

Debit Card: A card linked to your bank account, allowing you to spend only what you have.

Debt Consolidation: Combining multiple debts into one loan to lower interest or make payments manageable.

Debt Recovery: Pursuing unpaid debts, often through a collection agency.

Default: Failing to make payments as agreed, leading to penalties and credit score damage.

Deposit: Money put into an account, or an upfront payment, like for a house.

Direct Debit: Automatic payment method, allowing a company to take money regularly for bills.

Dividend: A payment made by a corporation to shareholders from profits.

Equity: Ownership value in an asset, minus remaining loans against it.

Fixed Interest Rate: Interest that stays the same throughout the term of the loan.

Guarantor: Someone who agrees to repay a loan if the borrower fails to do so.

Inflation: The rate of price rises for goods and services, affecting the cost of living.

Interest: Money paid by a borrower to a lender for using lent money, or earned on savings/investments.

Loan: Money borrowed to be repaid, typically with interest.

Minimum Payment: Smallest amount to pay on a credit card bill to keep the account in good standing.

Mortgage: A long-term loan to buy property, held as security against the loan.

Overdraft: A facility to withdraw more money than you have in an account, usually with fees and interest.

Pension: A long-term savings plan for retirement.

Repossession: When a lender takes back an item for defaulting on a loan.

Revolving Credit: A line of credit you can borrow against, repay, and then borrow against again.

Savings Account: An account for saving money, often with interest.

Secured Loan: A loan backed by collateral, often resulting in a lower interest rate.

Subprime Loan: A loan offered to those with poor credit histories, often with higher interest rates.

Tax: Mandatory charges imposed by the government to fund public services.

Variable Interest Rate: Interest that can change during the life of the loan, tied to an underlying benchmark.

Withdrawal: Taking money out of a bank account.

CONCLUSION

THIS IS THE BEGINNING OF SOMETHING GOOD.

The journey you've embarked on through this e-book is more than just a collection of facts, strategies, and concepts; it's a beginning, a starting point to reshape your financial future.

Financial literacy isn't about becoming an overnight expert. It's about empowering yourself with the knowledge and tools to take control of your money. Whether you're managing debt, exploring investment opportunities, or simply seeking to understand the financial world, what you've learned here is a foundation upon which you can build.

The relationship with money is multifaceted. It has practical aspects, emotional layers, and often intertwines with our daily lives in ways we might not even notice. Understanding this relationship can lead to a fulfilling and financially secure life.

Remember, the path to financial success is not a sprint but a marathon. It may seem daunting at first, but the keys are patience, persistence, and continuous learning. Embrace your financial journey with an open mind and a willing heart.

Make use of the practical tips, avoid common pitfalls, and reflect on the insights that resonate with you. Keep this e-book handy, refer back to it when needed, and don't hesitate to seek professional guidance if your situation requires it.

Above all, believe in yourself and your ability to create a thriving financial future. You've taken an important step by reading this, but the real adventure begins now. This is indeed the start of something good, and it's entirely in your hands.

Happy financial journeying!